VILLA D'ESTE

HADRIAN'S VILLA

TIVOLI - VILLA GREGORIANA

LOZZI *Roma*
edizioni turistiche

INDEX

Direzione e redazione:
LOZZI ROMA s.a.s.
Via Filippo Nicolai, 91 - 00136 ROMA
Tel. 06 35497051 - Tel. e Fax 06 35497074
lozzirm@spinweb.it

Stampato presso Tipografia Petruzzi C.
Zona Industriale Regnano
Città di Castello (PG)

Distribuzione:
INICOM s.r.l. - Tivoli

Entrance to the Villa.

VILLA D'ESTE

(The numbers in parenthesis beside each title refer to the map on page 63)

A BRIEF HISTORICAL SKETCH

Villa d'Este was conceived and commissioned by Ippolito d'Este II (1509-1572), Cardinal of Ferrara and son of the famous Lucrezia Borgia and Alfonso d'Este. His brilliant ecclesiastic and diplomatic career began at age ten, when he was named Archbishop of Milan. At age thirty, thanks to the support of King Francis I of France, to whose court Ippolito had represented the d'Este family for some time, Pope Paul III made him a cardinal.

At the Conclave of Julius III (1549-1550), d'Este was elected Governor of Tivoli. He believed that Tivoli's vicinity to the center of the temporal power of the Church would facilitate his ambitious plans for the future.
Ippolito D'Este took office on September 9th, 1550.
Accustomed as he was to the pomp and luxury of courtly life, he decided to build a new villa on the site to serve as a pleasant rustic retreat suitable for long private meetings. The Tivoli residence was to be a counterpart to the magnificent palace he had begun building at Monte Gior-

The fountain of the sleeping Venus.

dano in the center of Rome, which he intended to use for receptions and to sustain and foster valuable city friendships. This is how the Villa d'Este was born, and the new governor chose a spot with a lucky name: *"Valle Gaudente"* (the Valley of Pleasure-seeking).

Ippolito d'Este had at his disposal a great architect, Pirro Ligorio, and an enormous number of artists and craftsmen. Buildings and pathways materialized with a speed that would be considered modern even by today's standards.

The rapid completion of the work represented one of the few satisfactions for the Cardinal - the difficulties he encountered in political life, the plots woven against him and tiresome power struggles quickly laid to rest his aspirations to the papacy.

Ippolito D'Este died in 1572, attended to by only a few servants, after having been expelled from the State of the Church by Pope Paul IV following a conviction for simony. He was interred in the Church of Santa Maria Maggiore in Tivoli, which borders his beloved Villa.

The story of the Villa, however, does not end with the death of its founder, who bequeathed the Villa to the cardinals of the d'Este family. He was succeeded by Cardinal Luigi d'Este from 1572 to 1586, and then by Cardinal Alessandro d'Este until 1624. Both enriched the Villa with new fountains commissioned from the finest artists of the time; particularly notable was the contribution of Gian Lorenzo Bernini under Cardinal Alessandro.

The Villa d'Este then passed to the Habsburgs, to whom it remained until 1918, and suffered long periods of neglect due to the high costs of its upkeep. With the peace treaty that ended World War I, it became the property of the Italian State, and was completely restored.

Several bombs landed on the site during World War II, but repairs made immediately after the war restored the Villa to its previous condition.

THE ENTRANCE (1)

The original entrance to the Villa d'Este was on the old Via Tiburtina, at the foot of the hill upon which the Villa is built. The current entrance is on the side of the main building, an ex-Benedictine monastery which was first converted in 1256 into a Franciscan convent, and then into the Palace of the Governor of Tivoli. With brilliant structural modifications and additions, Pirro Ligorio gave the edifice new lines, and succeeded in creating what can be considered a true architectural gem.

The main facade of the mansion is on the side opposite the current entrance,

Throne Room.

Lower apartment - Central room ➡

which is on Piazza Santa Maria Maggiore.

The building forms a right angle with the 11th century Romanesque church of **Santa Maria Maggiore**, one side of which serves as a wall for the inner courtyard of the Villa.

The entrance gate belongs to the old Governor's Palace, and is surmounted by the coat of arms of Cardinal Carvajal, who restored the building while serving as governor. The entrance leads into a hall decorated with frescoes of biblical scenes; in a corner there is a stone plaque commemorating a visit by Pope Pius IX.

THE COURTYARD (2)

The entry hall leads to the old convent courtyard which Pirro Ligorio, with the help of the architect Raffaello da Firenze, magnificently adapted for the sumptuous residence of the Cardinal. A tuscan-style portico, supported by doric pilasters, runs along three sides of the courtyard. In the wall adjoining the Church of Santa Maria Maggiore, a fountain is framed in a play of perspective quite common to the late Renaissance. The water from the fountain falls into a basin made from an ancient sarcophagus. The fountain,

The Fountain of Tivoli.

The Room of Hercules.

Coffered ceiling in the Stanza da letto (Third Room).

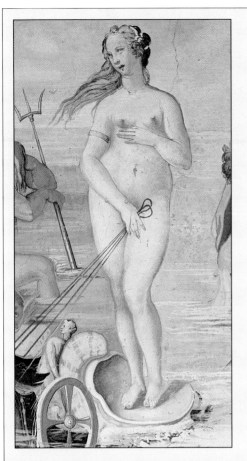

The birth of Venus

THE UPPER OR "OLD" APARTMENT

From the courtyard a double stairway leads to the upper floor, which was used as a private apartment by Cardinal Ippolito d'Este. The rooms are decorated with frescoes by Livio Agresti and a number of his pupils.

The most interesting rooms in the apartment are: the **Salone Centrale** (Central Room), also called the **Salone del Trono** (Throne Room), whose furniture and chandeliers come from the Reggia di Caserta; the nearby **Stanza da letto** (Third Room), bedroom of Cardinal Ippolito, with a beautiful coffered *ceiling* by the Flemish artist Flaminio Bollinger, decorated with the *d'Este coat of arms* and the Cardinal's own seal; followed by a room which probably served as a *library* and *private study*. Frescoes by Emilio Moretti of the emblems of the old arts and crafts guilds of Tivoli and other allegorical subjects decorate an old chapel on the way to the main Chapel, at the end of the left wing of the apartment.

The frescoes in the **Cappella** (Chapel) by Federico Zuccari and other artists represent the Prophets, Sybils and scenes from the life of the Madonna. Above the altar is the *Madonna di Reggio* (17th century), by Ludovico Agresti.

Turning back to the Salone Centrale, another five rooms (Sale VI-X) off to the right complete the picture gallery. The apartment has two terraces: one at the end of the corridor, with a view of the Roman countryside; the other, in the center of the Sala del Trono, looks onto the countryside of the Tibur valley, gently descending toward Rome. From the Cardinal's apartment two flights of wide stairs lead back down to the lower floor.

dedicated to Venus, is decorated with the figure of the sleeping goddess and with a 4th century bust, once thought to be the Emperor Constantine. The reliefs in the niche represent the spring on Monte Sant'Angelo, with the water descending to the Villa across rocks and vegetation revealing the beauty of the local landscape.

The Loggia of the Villa.

THE LOWER OR "NOBLE" APARTMENT

A corridor leads to the *Appartamento Inferiore*, or lower apartment, which served as the guest quarters, entering directly into the richly decorated **Salone Centrale** (Central Room), also known as the *Fontana di Tivoli* (Fountain of Tivoli). Set into a wall on the right is a fountain in mosaic, enamel and stucco that acts as a frame for a relief representing the so-called *Temple of the Sibyl of Tivoli*. The entire vault is decorated with frescoes, begun by Girolamo Muziano and fin-ished by Federico Zuccari (1542 - 1609) and his pupils. At the center of the vault, framed by a colonnade of bold perspec-tive, is *The Banquet of the Gods*, a fresco inspired by Raphael's painting in the Villa Farnesina in Rome. On the sides are images of the *sacrifices of Apollo, Ceres, Bacchus and Diana*. In the corners are four pairs of gods: *Bacchus and Ceres, Mars and Venus, Jove and Juno, Pallas and Mercury* . The halls to the right contain many inter-esting paintings of the principal events of the legendary origins of Tivoli. The frescoes in the **First Hall** are dedicated to the founding and construction of the

The Fountain of Bicchierone.

Coras and Tibertus against the Siculians; the *Imposition of the name Tiber* (derived from Tibertus) on the new city; and the *Victory of Hercules over the army of Albion*, won with the help of boulders hurled by Jove. The **Second Hall** contains a painting of *Phoebus racing in his chariot* (in the middle of the vault). Around this fresco and on the walls are images of the *Tibur*, the *Aniene* and the *spring at Albula*; the *Death of King Anius* ; the *Escape by sea of Ino* and her son Melicertus from her husband possessed by the Furies; the *Rescue of Ino* by Neptune, and her Arrival in Latium; and finally, the *Transformation of Ino into the Sibyl Albunea* at Tivoli.

The "Rometta", detail.

town, and are attributed to Cesare Nebbia and his pupils (1569). The main fresco in the middle of the vault shows *Catillus the Elder*, prefect of the fleet and General of Evander, *landing in Latium* and engaging in a battle with the natives. Four scenes surround this central image: in the first, *Catillus, Coras and Tibertus*, sons of Catillus the Elder; in the second, the *Fortune-tellers* replying to the three brothers, who had asked where to plough the first furrow to mark the site of the fortress; in the third, the *Erection of the walls of Tivoli*; in the fourth, the *Building of the houses*. The frescoes on the walls represent the *Struggle of Catillus*,

The "Rometta".

From there, two **Small Halls** with frescoes by Muziano and his school representing biblical scenes and landscapes. Off of the Central hall, a small covered loggia on the main facade offers the first marvelous views onto the garden. From the loggia a fine double flight of steps by Pirro Ligorio branches off to either side, leading down to a wide avenue. To the left, a set of arcades stretches out in the direction of the Roman countryside.

THE GARDEN

Narrow lanes bordered by symmetrical myrtle hedges descend from the avenue into this typically Italian garden, which is filled with thousands of trees and plants of all kinds. The garden is organized in a combination - original for the period - of terraces and downward slopes. One central longitudinal axis and five main transverse axes join the slopes and link

The d'Este coat of arms.

the various fountains situated at the edges of the Villa.

The garden - among the greatest in the country - is in perfect harmony with the Villa and its surroundings. Nature bursts forth in a grandiose and festive revelation of green tints and trees. For centuries these veils of water, spurting and iridescently splashing, placid fountains and opaline ponds have charmed visitors.

THE GROTTO OF DIANA (14)

At the end of the paths that lead to the left is the *Grotta di Diana*, decorated by Curzio Maccarone and Bolognese artists Lola and Paolo Calandrino with mosaics formed by scales of rock and stuccos in high and low relief. There are also remarkable decorations made from enamel, shells and coral.

The glazed majolica floor featured an array of colored figures. Some dates and names marked in rough letters are still visible: Portia, Nabuli, Amore were perhaps names of women who had been dear to the artisans who worked on the floor. Most of the precious sculptures that adorned the grotto are now in the Capitoline Museum in Rome, where they were placed after being acquired by Pope Benedict XIV; among those that remain are two statues of *Amazons*, *Minerva* and, notably, *Diana the Huntress* with her bow, to whom the grotto is dedicated.

Aside from the usual *Caryatids* and the rare stuccoed *quince branches*, the walls are embellished with mythological scenes featuring Minerva and Neptune.

THE BICCHIERONE (13)

The central axis of the Villa leads down to the calm and elegant fountain of the *Bicchierone* (large drinking glass), constructed in 1661 according to designs by Gian Lorenzo Bernini. The fountain, therefore, does not belong to the original plan of the Villa, but was added about a century later.

The exquisite architectural lines of the fountain, representing a fine chalice held up by a giant sea-shell, owes its particular charm to its harmonious and serene water play.

THE "ROMETTA" (15)

From the "Bicchierone", a cool avenue bordered by oaks and laurels turns off to the left and leads to the *"Rometta"*, a fantastic recreation of some of the most important buildings in ancient Rome. The large platform, supported by an impressive foundation, offers a fine perspective. It was designed by Pirro Ligorio and perhaps also by Ippolito II himself, and built in 1570 by fountain-maker Luzio Maccarone.

It is reached by a small bridge that spans a curving canal, in the middle of which,

The Hundred Fountains, by night.

The Hundred Fountains.

The Fountain of the Ovato, by night.

along a course representing the Tiber, there is a scale model of the Tiberina Island in Rome in the shape of an ancient Roman boat. The island was the site of a hospital and the uncoiling serpent alludes to Aesculapius, the god of medicine. The canal is formed by the confluence of two streams, representing the Tiber and the Aniene respectively, which come from the rocky wall in the background.

At the center of the Rometta is a statue of *Victorious Rome*, sculpted by Pietro Lamotte from a design by Ligorio, along with the *She-wolf* nursing the twins Romulus and Remus.

Today little remains of the original models, due to the passage of time and the fact that part of the ensemble (including the Colosseum, Capitol Hill, Pantheon and the Arch of Titus) was demolished. Nonetheless, the Rometta is still an expression of pure beauty as water gushes forth everywhere: in the air, on the ground, in the light and in the shadows.

THE HUNDRED FOUNTAINS (12)

When first built, the *Hundred Fountains* must have been particularly impressive: marble gleaming, sculptures intact, waters vigorous, inspiring in their sumptuousness, refinement and art. But no more - the marble is corroded and the trickling water reveals the patina of age. The Hundred Fountains border a long, straight path leading from the

"Rometta" fountain to the Fontana dell'Ovato. The water falls into three long parallel channels arranged one above the other, forming one single water play.

Allegorically, the thin spurts of water, fed by the hundred jets, represent the Aniene river which runs from Tivoli to Rome, where it flows into the Tiber. Hanging above the highest channel are sculptures of *lilies, obelisks, boats and eagles*, all the Cardinal's beloved symbols: the lilies represent unforgettable France, the boats St. Peter, and the obelisks unfulfilled papal power. The eagle belonged to the coat of arms of the d'Este family.

Pirro Ligorio designed the 100 meter-long path, and was responsible for the two orders of overlapping basins on the uphill side.

THE FOUNTAIN OF "OVATO" (8)

Coming from the Hundred Fountains and walking past the "Bollori" stairs and the Fountain of the Dragons (see below) to the left, the path leads to the *Fountain of the Ovato*, also known as the Fountain of Tivoli, built by Pirro Ligorio. The canal that brought the water of the Aniene river to the Villa once flowed nearby.

The fountain takes its name from its egg-

The Fountain of the Ovato.

The Fountain of the Ovato. The Sibyl of Tibur.

bordered by a half-moon terrace with a marble balustrade overhanging the mighty and crystal-clear flow of water that drops down in a resonating dome. The basin below is lined by a semi-circle of pilasters which form of a nymphaeum. In the niches statues of nymphs hold vases from which water flows. This is the work of Giovan Battista della Porta, inspired by Pirro Ligorio. In the middle of the basin there is a large shell with open valves; the parapet of the basin is lined with lively ceramics featuring details of the d'Este coat of arms. Opposite the fountain there are tables with Roman feet and two stucco statues in their own niches. Centuries-old plane trees embellish the scene.

Though perhaps not a perfect all-around work, the *Fountain of the "Ovato"* is admirable for its general harmony and its profusion of ornamental motifs which often served as inspiration to numerous artists.

like, oval shape, and it is perhaps the most typically baroque fountain in the Villa. The fountain appears particularly elaborate, thanks to the profusion of rocks and ornamental boulders which Curzio Maccarone showered upon it in order to convey the wild atmosphere of Mount Helicon.

The *Pegasus* (winged horse) atop the fountain is placed so well that it seems truly about to soar into the air.

A good ways down the central axis is a simple statue of the *Sibyl of Tibur* (Sibyl Albunea) holding the hand of her son Melicerte, symbolizing Tivoli. The statue is the work of the Flemish sculptor Giglio della Vellita. On either side are marble figures by Giovanni Malanca representing the *Aniene and Herculanean rivers*.

The tall, rocky part of the fountain is

The Fountain of "Ovato". The Aniene.

The small waterfall of the Fountain of the Ovato.

The Fountain of the Organ.

THE FOUNTAIN OF THE ORGAN (27)

A shady and attractive lane to the left leads to a clearing where stands the *Fountain of the Organ*, so named because it was once connected to a water-driven mechanism that imitated the sounds of an organ.

The fountain consists of a large structure designed by Pirro Ligorio along baroque lines. A large oval basin at the base of the fountain is encircled by a lovely balustrade in mixed style. An apse opens at the center of the fanciful structure; four colossal rough-hewn Telamones by Pirrin del Gagliardo support the sides of the mock arch; and above there are multi-colored stucco panels depicting mythological scenes with Orpheus, Marsius, Apollo and others.

A profusion of ornamental motifs stretches across the facade, including abundant grotesque coats of arms, flowers, sirens, winged victories and seashells. In the middle, beneath the apse, there is a delightful and beautifully proportioned *opening*, designed by Bernini to house the Hydraulic Organ.

The Hydraulic Organ, for which the fountain was originally named, was the ingenuous creation of Claude Venard, and was once one of the wonders of the Villa. Water dropped through a conduit into an underground cavity, forcing a strong draft of air through the organ pipes. Another heavy jet of water slowly rotated a toothed copper cylinder mounted on an iron frame which moved the keys of the organ, playing madrigals and motets. The listeners found it difficult to believe that the music came from a simple hydraulic mechanism and not a band of hidden musicians.

THE FOUNTAIN OF THE DRAGONS (24)

The shady path to the right of the Fountain of the Ovato leads to the *Fountain of the Dragons (or the Fountain of the Girandola)*, the dominant motif at the very heart of the Villa's garden.

This is a fascinating fountain, at the center of which is a group of four horrid dragons "with wings and open mouths of the kind that frighten those who look upon them," executed, according to legend, in just one night in September 1572, when Pope Gregory XIII (whose coat of arms featured dragons) was a guest at the Villa. Previously, it had been called the *Fountain of the Girandola* (rotating fireworks) for its complicated waterworks by Tommaso da Siena, which produced a rapid succession of explosions, cannon shots and blasts which resembled fireworks, like those that were set off at Castel Sant'Angelo in Rome.

Recently several of the spouts have been restored, crowning the mighty jet of water which roars skyward, filling the air with resounding pistol cracks. This fountain was designed and built by

The Fountain of the Organ.

The Fountain of Dragons.

Pirro Ligorio, who as usual created first and foremost a large, impressive architectural structure.

The two harmonious staircases that embrace the fountain bring the separate levels and perspectives into balance. Apart from its architectural significance, this particularly vivacious and graceful fountain is also a sculptural gem.

FOUNTAIN OF THE OWL (22)

To the left of the Fountain of the Dragons is the *Fountain of the Owl* (or of the "Birds"), a famous attraction designed by Giovanni di Luca from Burgundy and built by the Florentine Raffaele Sangallo. By means of a complicated mechanism and various water jets, swarms of metallic birds suddenly appeared on bronze branches which were woven through the niches of the fountain, singing in the sonorous tones of the flute and the ocarina. At a certain moment, a mechanical owl jumped out, shrieking its unwelcome cry. The hydraulic apparatus was constructed by fountain-maker Luc Le Clerc, but all that is left today are the enthusiastic descriptions of the writers of the period.

Among other losses are a mosaic in the central nymphaeum, several high reliefs, stuccos, and the Roman statues and groups of Fauns and Satyrs by Ulisse Macciolini da Volterra.

THE FOUNTAIN OF PROSERPINA (21)

Architecturally similar to the Fountain of the Owl, the *Fountain of Proserpina* was designed (like the Fountain of the Dragon) to bring together two separate levels of the Villa.

Created as an open-air dining room, the fountain is composed of a central nymphaeum flanked by two niches enclosed by four twisted columns and bounded by two staircases which join the different levels of the park. On the whole, the structure is well-balanced. The fountain takes its name from the marble sculpture in the center of the

Fountain of the Dragons.

nymphaeum depicting Proserpina being kidnapped from Avernus by Pluto. Two Silenes play marine harps while a pair of Dolphins stir up the water. This early 17th century marble group, together with the twisted columns sumptuously decorated with vines and tiny cherubs, was regarded as one of the most exquisite baroque scenes in the Villa. Unfortunately, it is in poor condition.

THE FISH PONDS (30)

A bit further downhill are the *Fish Ponds*, made up of three large rectangular basins arranged in a row, bordered by lush vegetation and animated by thin jets which spring from the vases that decorate the balustrades.

At the time of their construction, the *fish ponds* served as a breeding ground for choice species of fish. Nearby, luxurious

The Owl Fountain.

kiosks were built for those who wanted to rest during a stroll or for those who needed fishing tackle in order to catch the fish. In this way the guests of the Cardinal not only enjoyed healthy surroundings and the enchanting waters of the fountains, but could also have the pleasure of catching fresh water fish out of the ponds. Snow-white swans glided over the water, while ducks fought with the trout and pikes for the bread crumbs strewn by the hands of the Cardinal.

Fountain of Neptune with the Fish Ponds.

The Fountain of Neptune, by night.

THE FOUNTAIN OF NEPTUNE (28)

At the end of the lanes which border the fish ponds is the *Fountain of Neptune*, which forms a marvelous background for this enchanting spot.

Without a doubt the grandest fountain in the Villa, the *Fountain of Neptune* was built in the 1920's by Attilio Rossi, then the Honorable Curator of the Villa d'Este, who - with rare artistic sensitivity - succeeded in boldly grafting several water displays onto Pirro Ligorio's original waterfall, which had belonged to the nearby Hydraulic Organ.

The fountain appears to grow smoothly out from the large base, gradually intensifying and becoming ever more lively as it climbs up to join the balustrade of the Hydraulic Organ. The symmetrical jets hurl skyward in a fluid pyramidal pattern that brings to mind a vision of vibrating organ pipes.

In front of the basin of the fountain there are several rectangular patches of flowers and grass. All the water comes from above, dropping down on its own or shooting from numerous spurts. Immediately underneath the balustrade lie three connected nymphaeums.

The compact and thundering mass of the water from the cascade falls onto the central axis of the nymphaeums and the *Hydraulic Organ*, composing the driving *leit-motif* of the entire fountain.

At the base of the nymphaeums sits a large terrace-basin from which twelve strong jets shoot water at different heights tapering from the center toward the sides. The middle of the terrace-basin has a deep recess to catch the pre-cipitous waters of the cascade which break into a foaming white cloud on a fourth, lower nymphaeum. The main portion of which juts out boldly to break the fall of the water and to inter-rupt the considerable difference in the levels of the terrace-basin above and the basins at the base of the fountain.

Part of the cascade and some of the overflow from the terrace-basin are col-lected by a large basin below the lowest

The Fountain of the Pegasus.

The Fountain of Ariadne.

nymphaeum, from which two gigantic jets on either side send water shooting skyward. The basin is divided in two by the nymphaeum.

Immediately below lie other basins, each slightly lower than the previous one. The sparkling water flows peacefully from one basin to the next, skimming the marble rims like placid and gentle rapids.

The lowest basins ingeniously serve to calm the impetuous waters of the cascade and jets, calming their flow to suit the tranquil Fish Ponds - thus a tumultuous foaming torrent is gradually transformed into an emerald stretch of water mirroring the peaceful sky above. In the lowest nymphaeum stands a giant bust of Neptune, designed by Pirro Ligorio.

MINOR FOUNTAINS (31-36)

Apart from the fountains already described, there are several more worth mentioning: though no longer adorned by its original statuary, the graceful *Fountain of Ariadne* (36) retains all of its simple charm, situated on the panoramic side of the park overlooking the Roman countryside; the two fountains of the *Mete Sudanti*, which are modeled on the Meta Sudans in Rome (located near the Colosseum), shed tears of water in humble silence; four small basins destined for the fish ponds; the unrecognizable *Fountain of the d'Este Eagles*, almost entirely crumbled away; a grotto with a rough statue of a prophet made in plaster in the 18th century; and finally, ruins of a Roman house.

The Fountain of the Neptune.

THE FOUNTAIN OF NATURE (34)

The only other fountain of interest is the *Fountain of Nature*, standing against a wall near the Villa's original entrance, with a *Statue of Nature* taken from the Fountain of the Hydraulic Organ. The work of Giglio della Vellita, it is a likeness of the many-breasted Diana of Ephesus, which symbolized the eternally fecund nature and unstoppable flow of life. The workmanship of the statue is rather rough, but the expressive northern features somehow capture a bit of life's mystery and solitude.

The Fountain of Nature.

THE ROTUNDA
OF THE CYPRESSES (33)

Gripping the ground firmly with their enormous roots, svelte cypresses soar upward, scraping the clouds, mighty symbols of the triumph of nature. Some of the most majestic of them crown a round space called the *Rotunda of the* *Cypresses*, which opens onto the main axis of the Villa.

Around the rotunda are four low fountains with triple basins in travertine. In front, the central staircase cuts straight up the hill to the facade of the Villa.

From here, a single glance can take in one of the most beautiful and encompassing views of the Villa d'Este with its varied architectural beauty.

The Rotunda of the Cypresses.

The Fountain of Neptune. ➡

TIVOLI

Tivoli is reached by *Via Tiburtina*, the ancient Roman consular road which takes its name from Tivoli itself.

The town was called Tibur in Roman times after the legendary Tibertus, venerated as founder of the city with his brother Catillus. The latter gave his name to the hill which dominates Tivoli, rising on the right bank of the Aniene river.

Set atop the first pre-Appennine buttress which suddenly rears up after the vast expanse of the Roman plain, Tivoli occupies a wonderful panoramic position. After traveling along the winding Via Tiburtina that climbs up the green,

Gian Lorenzo Bernini's Baptism of Christ.

Panorama of Tivoli.

olive-clad hill, the large *Piazza Garibaldi*, bordered on the left by a spacious panoramic terrace, offers views onto the entire plain and Rome in the distance.

Tivoli is best known for its three villas (Villa d'Este, Hadrian's Villa and Villa Gregoriana), yet the city is rich with several other interesting monuments and sites that are worth visiting, if only in passing.

The distinguished monuments scattered through the town, their panoramic position, and the waters of the Aniene river, seemingly omni-present in waterfalls, cascades and conduits for industrial use, help create the intimate surroundings for the villas.

A brief itinerary begins at Piazza Garibaldi, at the end of which, on the left, is Piazza Trento. Here rises the Church of **Santa Maria Maggiore**

The Deposition from the Cross.

(known to locals as San Francesco), a beautiful 13th-century Romanesque-Gothic building. From Piazza Trento, nearby Via della Missione leads towards the old part of town, with its medieval quarter and Romanesque-Gothic churches.

Narrow undulating streets and picturesque **medieval houses** on Via Campitelli and Piazza San Nicola are a pleasantly surprising feature of this small town.

From here, Via del Colle leads to the Romanesque Church of **San Silvestro**, with particularly noteworthy 12th and 13th-century frescoes in the apse.

Further down is the **Duomo**, dedicated to San Lorenzo, rebuilt in the middle of the 17th century. Highlights include the fine *portico* and the Romanesque *campanile* (12th century).

Inside is an expressive *Deposition from the Cross* (one of the most famous wood sculptures of the 13th century) and the equally important *Tryptich of the Savior*, kept in an embossed silver casing, a valuable piece of silver-craftsmanship that dates to 1449.

The Duomo closes one of the short sides of what was once the Forum - the center of public and private life in the city - during Roman times, as evidenced by the many important relics found in the area. Going towards the Aniene, at the level of Ponte Gregoriano, is Piazza Rivarola. From there, Via della Sibilla goes left to one of the most famous monuments in Tivoli, the so-called *Temple of the Sibyl*. The true name of the temple is not known, though it is thought to have been dedicated to Vesta, or else to Hercules Saxanus, who was particularly venerated in Tivoli.

The adjacent rectangular temple was probably the one dedicated to the Sibyl.

The temples rise from a rocky footing, overhanging the romantic park of *Villa Gregoriana*.

ROCCA PIA

The Rocca, an imposing 15th century fortress, owes its name to Pope Pius II, who had it constructed as a perpetual warning to the quarrelsome and proud people of Tivoli, who were far from docile subjects.

At the corners of the quadrilateral fortress, there are four massive cylin-

Church of St. Mary Major

Medieval Tivoli.

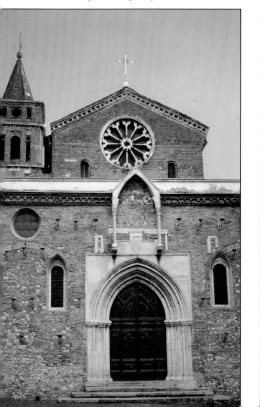

drical towers, two of which date to the time of Pius II, while the other two were added by Alessandro VI at the beginning of the 16th century.

Its unadorned, severe beauty makes the fortress a true masterpiece of its kind, deserving of recognition especially because its ponderous walls have stood witness to important historical events. It was here that the Popes of the 15th and 16th centuries loved to take long summer vacations, accompanied by their dignitaries and numerous artists who were working for the Papal Court, such as Michelangelo, Raphael and the great musician Pierluigi da Palestrina. It was during one of these usual periods of relaxation at Rocca Pia, in September of 1539, that Pope Paul II approved the first five chapters of the Society of Jesus which were read to him by the founder St. Ignatius of Loyola.

Rocca Pia.

VILLA GREGORIANA

From the center of town, the entrance to the Villa is off the road that leads to the railroad station, just past Ponte Gregoriano.

Built on the precipices of the Aniene river and the fluvial slopes of Monte Catillo, the Villa was named after Pope Gregory XVI, who had re-routed the destructive river in 1835, rendering its rage harmless.

Inside, myrtle-bordered lanes, rocky paths, worn steps, steep lanes and tiny tunnels wind through woods thick with giant trees, past ancient ruins, along the edges of dizzying precipices and through glades drenched in sunlight.

Beyond the entrance, signs mark a path to the right that leads to the mouths of several tunnels which channel the Aniene river to the Villa's *large waterfall*.

Ruins of the Villa of Manilo Vopisco, Roman Consul in 114 AD.

The Aniene Watefall.

and since then the Aniene's waters have not posed a threat. The drop from the tunnels totals over 360 feet, and though the flow was once very forceful, it has decreased significantly since a hydroelectric power plant was installed upstream.

When on occasion the flow is increased, the waterfall and its splendid surroundings again become among the most impressive in Italy. A rough path leads down a few dozen yards to the so-called *Horseshoe*, a terrace that juts out, precariously close to the waterfall. From this point you can admire the whirling mass of water that seems to fall directly overhead, but instead tumbles harmlessly amid a deafening roar into the dancing waves far below, over which a veil of white water dust is permanently spread.

Turning back, a lane descends to the central part of the Villa and the Canal of the Stipa or Bernini's outlet (so-called because the great architect restored it in 1669). It was once used as an overflow channel when the Aniene flooded. Nearby are the *Grottos of Neptune and the Sirens*. Over centuries, the forceful waters of the river gradually wore away the rocks, forming impressive caverns. The higher *Grotto of Neptune* was partly destroyed by a flood in 1836, but the *Grotto of the Sirens*, below, is rich in stalactites and tiny cascades.

In 1832, Pope Gregory XVI had the architect Clemente Folchi build the tunnels in order to avoid a repetition of the disastrous flood of 1826, in which many people were killed and buildings destroyed. The challenging construction of the tunnels was successfully completed in 1835,

At the top of the opposite slope is the Galleria Miollis, a small tunnel with windows carved out of the rock by the French General Miollis, governor of Rome in 1809.

It is worth noting that at the entrances to the tunnels (outside the Villa), excavations during construction in 1832-1835 revealed a *cemetery* with various monuments and marble slabs which date to the Roman Empire, ruins of the ancient Bridge of Valerius and of the aqueduct which brought water from the Aniene to the *villa of Manlius Vopiscus*, who served as a Roman consul in 114 AD. Highly praised in the verses of the Roman poet Stazio, the few visible *ruins* that remain suggest the magnificence of the original structures.

TEMPLE OF VESTA

The temple is round, like all those dedicated to Vesta, which were meant to symbolize the earth. It stands near what is believed to be the temple of the Sibyl Albunea, situated in the heart of the Tiburtina Acropolis.

The late Republican structure was restored, as recorded on the architrave, by Lucius Gellius, magistrate and curator of public works in Tivoli in the first century AD. Subsequently, the temple was made into a Christian church, but was restored to its original form at the end the 19th century.

It was once topped by a rather low cupola, on the top of which a large opening let out the smoke from the sacred fire. A

The Temple of Vesta and view of Tivoli.

small circular roof over the vent hole prevented the rain from coming in. It is Corinthian in style and has a peristyle of grooved columns. The base is covered in slabs of travertine. The architrave features a lovely, delicately worked frieze, composed of floral garlands, cups, heads of bulls, roses, bunches of grapes, sprigs of grain and fruit. The coffered ceiling of the portico was entirely decorated with a double row of roses at the center of each panel.

The stunning view from the temple encompasses the Aniene's precipes as well as the gentle slopes of Tivoli's hills, clad in olive grooves. Seen from a distance, the temple fits the surrounding landscape so well that it appears to have sprung up from the earth to remain forever part of it.

Temple of Vesta.

HADRIAN'S VILLA

(See the map on page 60)

When Publius Elis Hadrian assumed power on the 2nd of August, 117 AD, the Roman empire was at its maximum extent and power. The second Spanish-born Roman Emperor (after Trajan) Hadrian was a wise politician and a first-rate military commander. Despite numerous victories, he understood that Rome's conquering period had come to an end, and that the empire needed stability above all else.

Perhaps the most complex and compelling of all Roman emperors, Hadrian was a highly-cultured man. He appreciated all forms of art, but had a special passion for architecture, which he indulged even while traveling. In England, Hadrian rebuilt London in 122 AD, about sixty years after the fire, and he also constructed the famous *Vallum*, a long defensive wall that was named after him. In Athens, where he spent much of his time trying to strengthen Rome's eastern boundaries against the incipient threat of barbarian invasion, the emperor carried out conspicuous restoration projects and enriched the city with new buildings of great beauty. Hadrian understood the strongest cultural and civil needs of his time, and brought

The Canopus with the Caryatids.

together the refinements of Greek culture and the traditional governing skills which the Romans had developed over the centuries. This combination was embodied in the Villa he built. The charming mix of ruins and natural landscape makes it a powerful romantic attraction, and the deeply innovative nature of Hadrian's architecture is self-evident in each building.

This extraordinary complex was constructed between the years 118 and 134 A.D. at the foot of Tibur - today's Tivoli - a town founded in the 9th century BC on the border of the calcareous terrace stretching from the Tiburtini Hills toward the Roman countryside. Four years after the completion of the Villa, the emperor died at age 62 from cirrhosis of the liver in Baia, where he had gone seeking mild weather and a cure for the disease.

It is difficult to imagine the scope of the original Villa; only one fifth of the three-hundred hectares that originally occupied the site are visible today.

Among Villa Adriana's best-known features are the numerous references to those places that had most impressed the emperor's memory and spirit, which are mentioned in a list by Elio Sparziano, one of the writers of the Historia Augusta. But only the Canopus, as we will see below, can be identified with one of these places. All the other names were suggested by Renaissance or later scholars. Modern scholars tend to recognize the mark of Hadrian's political program, which for the first time put the provinces on par with Rome, in the Villa's bizarre and even capricious reproductions of exotic architecture. But in reality, the designs employed were more a matter of personal interpretation than of mere imitation. Hadrian's immediate successors, the Antonini, used the Villa as their summer residence, but after them the Villa fell into disrepair. Diocletian restored it at the end of the 3rd century AD. Shortly afterwards, according to several texts, Constantine embellished Constantinople - the new capital of the eastern empire - with many artistic pieces taken from Villa Adriana, which from that time shared with most of the great Roman monuments a destiny of neglect and damage (Gothic and Byzantine armies alternatively camped in the Villa's grounds during the terrible Gothic wars) and even more devastating pillages in the 16th century, during the first archaeological excavations.

About 300 masterpieces have so far been discovered and put on display in museums and collections all over the world. Some of these works definitely deserve mention, if only to imagine how they might have once adorned the Villa.

Among Roman copies from Greek originals: the famous *Discobolus of Mirone*, housed in the Vatican Museums, and the *Tyrannicides* at the Naples' National Museum (5th century BC); Praxitele's *Three resting satyrs*, one of which is displayed at the Capitoline Museums in Rome (4th century BC). Unforgettable sculptures from the 3rd to the 1st centuries BC are the *Niobide* (Vatican Museums), the *Crouching Venus* by Doidaldas (Museo Nazionale Romano, Rome), the *Two Centaurs with Faun* in *rosso antico* marble (Capitoline Museums) and a Faun (Vatican Museums). Several original Roman sculptures such as the *Colossal masks and the Ocean*, *Two telamons*, *Two peacocks*, a *Deer's head* and, above all, the gigantic *Antinoos* represented like Bacchus, are also on display at the Vatican Museums. Of remarkable interest is the large group of sculptures made in the Egyptian style, divided between the Vatican Museums and the Capitoline Museums. Finally, some splendid mosaics include: the *Mosaic of the doves* at the Capitoline Museums and the noteworthy collection at the Vatican Museums, which includes the panels with Animals, in the Room of the Animals; the *Theater masks*, which gave the name to the famous Gabinetto; and the cheerful *Flower garlands* in the library.

THE ENTRANCE TO THE VILLA: THE POECILE (2)

Today the entrance to the Villa is through an opening in the wall (about 9 meters high) which was once completed by porticoes on both sides and marked a great rectangular space (232 x 97 meters). The original lake at the center has been restored. It could be that this was the Poecile, from the name of the Painted Portico in Athens which Hadrian had greatly admired, though other theories suggest that it may have been a hippodrome.

The semicircular nymphaeum of the Canopus.

The Wall of the Poecile.

BUILDING WITH THREE EXEDRAS (4)

Standing outside the exit on the longest side of the Poecile is one of Hadrian's most extraordinary projects. Because the purpose of this structure is unknown, it's simply referred to as *Building with three exedras*, an excellent example of Hadrian's architectural innovations, this clover-shaped building features curved walls around a central plan.

THE SMALL THERMAE (5)

Three splendid baths were available to the guests and the personnel of the Villa. Probably reserved for women, the *Small Thermae* were rendered no less harmonious by their size. They show imaginative innovations such as a singular *octagonal room*, or the external wall on the northern side, which, with its light and shade effects was considered a source of inspiration for one of the major exponents of Baroque architecture, Francesco Borromini. The typical structure of Roman baths included a *frigidarium* (cold water bath) and a *calidarium* (hot water bath). The octagonal room, with a 10.5 meters dome, served as the *tepidarium*, which was filled with warm water. In addition there was a large pool with two apses flanked by marble steps and small rooms, used not only for workouts, massages and gymnastics, but also for lectures and relaxation.

THE GREAT THERMAE (6)

Separated from the Small Thermae by a courtyard, the *Great Thermae* are stunning in their solemn grandiosity. Though difficult to recognize at first glance, the structure corresponds to the standard plan of Roman baths. The large rectangular space in the back was the *open-air gym*, where the workout began with some exercises; adjacent was an enclosed chamber called *sphaeristerium* for games with a ball. The nearby rectangular space in the center served as dressing room and led to the *calidarium*, or hot bath in three pools, on the right. Back toward the Small Thermae was the *tepidarium*, or tepid bath, followed by the *laconicum*, a large round hall with an apse for taking hot-air saunas (there were no hydraulic mechanisms); continuing toward the rear, separated by some service areas, was a hall with apses for the *frigidarium*: the cold water pools which were the final part of the laborious hygiene rituals of the baths, an essential part of the daily life of the ancient Romans. The surprisingly efficient and particularly ingenious heating system produced humid heat, with steam from the great boilers, and also dry heat from air columns directly heated by wood-burning ovens. The hot air and vapor circulated in special double chambers (*sospensurae*) under the floor and by means of narrow canals which ran inside the walls. To the right down the lane stand the scarce remains of a building of uncertain use, called the **Vestibule** (7).

The lake of the Poecile.

THE CANOPUS (8)

The great supply of water was one of the leading factors that ultimately convinced Hadrian to select this site for his Villa. Water plays the chief role in the *Canopus*, the most celebrated part of the complex. Reflections of some of the ruins of Hadrian's architectural fantasies, shimmer in water in the long basin (119 m. x 18 m.) set in the small buttressed valley. The name Canopus - the only certain one among all the structures of the Villa - recalls an Egyptian settlement near modern Abukir, a town not far from Alexandria, celebrated in antiquity for its magnificence. But for Hadrian, the site remained sadly linked to the memory of his beloved Antinoos, who drown himself there. Some of the sculpted portraits of this beautiful, effeminate youth were found in the Canopus - their reflections in the water recalling the mythological Narcissus, also a symbol of an inextricable, tragic combination of beauty, youth and death.

According to Strabone, author of "Geographia", considered to have been one of the most noteworthy tourist guides in antiquity, the original Canopus was decidedly different from Hadrian's Canopus.

The latter shows its architectural high point in the *semicircular nymphaeum*, whose back wall appears animated by a central niche flanked by smaller niches, above which rises a segmented cupola. This theme is repeated in different dimensions elsewhere in the architecture of the Villa. Recent excavations have identified it as a grand *triclinium* (dining room), used for parties and solemn banquets in summertime.

Castings of four *caryatids* (female statues with capitals above their heads used in the place of columns), which were themselves excellent copies of the famous originals on the Erechtheion in Athens, were placed along one of the sides of the canal along with two *Silenuses* (the originals are in the nearby museum).

MUSEUM OF THE CANOPUS (9)

Located in the ancient structures of the "tabernae" that border part of the little Canopus valley, the museum is an interesting structure in and of itself, built in pure Roman style. Most of the works on display come from the Canopus, where corresponding castings now stand. Particularly remarkable are: *four Caryatids* over two meters tall, in pristine condition, notably better preserved than the well-known originals in Athens; *two*

The Large Thermae. The Frigidarium.

Silenuses bearing capitals in the shape of a basket over their heads in a caryatid-like fashion, whose castings are on the right bank of the Canopus; *Mars, Mercury and Athena*, excellent Roman copies from 5th century BC Greek originals, whose castings are placed under the graceful Canopo's arches; the oldest existent copy of the *Amazon of Pheidias* and a fine replica of the *Amazon of Polykleitos*; the *Nile and the Tiber*, represented like half-laid male figures; a *Crocodile* in cipollino marble, in the mouth of which the once spouting pipe is still visible. Some *marble male busts*; numerous *columns and pillars* decorated with naturalistic motifs and various decorative fragments. The copy of the *Venus of Knidos* (4th century BC), worthy of the better-known Greek original kept in the Vatican Museums.

To the left of the entrance to the Canopus stands the most massive building of Hadrian's Villa, the **Praetorium** (10), a tall edifice which was used for services.

THE THREE PERISTYLES OF THE IMPERIAL PALACE

Back towards the Canopus and to the right are the so-called *Great Peristyles*. This area is the very heart of the Villa: between the Poecile and the Thermae is Hadrian's residence, which is organized in three sections, each with a roofed porticoe or peristyle.

The first and best-known peristyle is the **Piazza d'oro** (Golden Square) (11), celebrated for the prominence of its stunning architectural design. It is a large, nearly square-shaped (51x60 m.) atrium on the northeast end of the Villa, with a double portico which, on the open side, is sup-ported by sixty alternating granite and cipollino marble columns. Stuccoed half-columns made of bricks once stood on the opposite side against the back wall of the portico. On the southeastern side was the octagonal *Imperial Room*, formed by alternating convex and concave walls. This led to the adjoining rooms, once decorated with exquisite marble friezes only partially visible today. Nothing remains of the bold dome that rested on the convex walls. The *Vestibule* on the northeastern end of the Golden Square also has an octagonal plan. Large semi-circular niches alternate with rectangular ones on all but the two north and south sides, which were left open to be used as passageways. The rather well-preserved segmented *dome* has a central window and is supported by eight columns. Inside the Vestibule are some of the best floor mosaics in the Villa, with all their "tesserae" perfectly arranged in geometrical patterns reminiscent of oriental rugs. This first peristyle is quite far from the imperial residence, a complex of buildings set out by the outline of the **Quadriporticus with Fish Pond** (12), laid against the slopes of the low hill. The fish pond features carefully crafted details such as niches carved out of the wall at the bottom for seating the imperial guests who indulged in catching fish. On the front side of the mighty building, large panoramic terraces open onto the spacious Roman countryside. Other landmarks in the shade of Hadrian's apartments are the Poecile, the Building with three exedras and, right below the terraces of the Quadriporticus, a rectangular **Nymphaeum** (13) that was once believed to be a stadium. Behind this first complex and past the **Firemen's Barracks**

The Canopus.

The Canopus. Detail with the Statue of Mars.

The Golden Square.

(14) is the area in which Hadrian exercised his imperial authority. Careful restoration has restored the original, elegant solemnity to a corner of the **Room of the Doric Pilasters** (15), with clean and straight lines set against the more curvaceous surroundings. Hadrian's personal touch is recognizable in the extraordinary height of the pilasters rounded off by an impressive barrel vault, which was a great innovation on the Doric order. The room has a basilican form, and was likely used as a tribunal. The adjoining **Nymphaeum** (16) features one of the Villa's infinite innovative architectural designs based on curved rather than straight lines. The large **Peristyle of the imperial palace** (17), originally a portico supported by brick columns, is visible, but the palace itself is for the most part unexcavated.

Among the areas that have so far been recognized are: the **Summer Triclinium** (18), the **Private Library** (19), the **Room with Three Naves** (20), and the **Cryptoporticus** (21), which belonged to an enormous network of underground tunnels.

Between the Peristyle and the nearby **Thermae with Heliocaminus** (22), mentioned above, there is a small olive tree grove above what is evidently an archaeological site of primary importance, believed to contain ruins similar in struc-

Room of the Doric pilasters.

ture to those of the thermae joining the palace. The word *heliocaminus* (literally, "sun heater") refers to the large circular room at one corner which houses a large round basin. Five huge windows in the south-west wall suggest that solar energy was used for heating. The device that produced hot air was fed by three big stoves placed in the external basement-like ambulatory dug around the room. From there, the hot air filtered inside the room through countless grooves made in the walls, providing constant and uniform heat even when the sun wasn't warm enough - a clever and surprisingly modern strategy of drawing energy from different sources. From the severe, dry heat produced in this unusual room, totally without hydraulic pipes of any sort, one passed to the *frigidarium* for a cold bath, an ample space in the open air, exposed to the northeast.

At the center of a courtyard surrounded by a triporticus supported by columns in gray granite was a large pool with an average depth of 1,40 meters. The sides of the pool were decorated with alternating round and rectangular niches and little fountains. In bad weather, a semi-circular marble basin was available for cold baths inside a large sheltered room in the adjoining courtyard. The usual service rooms completed the elegant and functional structure.

The Villa of the Island (formerly the Maritime Theater).

The third peristyle is the **Library Courtyard** (23), an ample square (65x52 m.) built in the early phase of the construction of the Villa for Hadrian's wife, the empress Sabina. The name comes from the nearby **Greek Library** (27) and **Latin Library** (28), a pair of peculiar, vertical edifices identified as summer triclinums. Beyond this courtyard, there are other interesting buildings, noticeably the Praetorians' quarters, also called **Hospitalia** (24), with about ten bedrooms; one of the many **tricliniums** (25) scattered on the grounds of the Villa; and, finally, the **Pavillion of Tempe** (26), a panoramic terrace looking out onto a landscape which is no longer untouched.

THE VILLA OF THE ISLAND (29), ONCE CALLED THE MARITIME THEATER

A few steps from the west side of the Library Courtyard is the most unique and, along with the Canopus, best-known structure of Hadrian's Villa. Here, too, water plays the chief role: a moat encircles a tiny island, upon which is a little villa formed by a series of differently designed rooms, all arranged around a small courtyard with porticoes and a fountain with convex sides. The moat is surrounded with a corridor-like portico with forty Ionic columns placed on a low wall. Access to the island was via two

The Statue of Venus.

wooden drawbridges (now there's a brick bridge instead) which extended only from the island and slid on mechanical wheels which left visible tracks on the bottom of the moat.

Because it is not mentioned in the written records referring to Hadrian or his Villa, scholars have suggested a wide variety of descriptions and purposes for this original and complex, yet architecturally rigorous structure. After dropping the traditional name of Maritime Theater, interpretations of the structure range from the ordinary - that the villa was nothing more than a pleasant retreat, to the fascinating hypothesis that identifies the building with a sort of sanctuary used to host the divine emperor in a "cosmic theater", featuring a planetarium-like ceiling.

Interestingly, the total dimensions of the structure, moat and corridor match exactly those of the Pantheon in Rome (44 m.), which was rebuilt by Hadrian himself.

Some of the ruins in the peripheral areas can provide visitors interested in a longer walk with a more in-depth understanding of the essence of the Villa, based on the fusing together of architecture and nature. An uphill path starting at the Museum of the Canopus leads to the panoramic **Torre di Roccabruna** (30) and to the ruins of the **Accademia** (32-33).

On the opposite side of the Villa there's a group of sparse buildings. In a clearing surrounded by trees stands a **Small Circular Temple** (34) with Doric columns, reconstructed in 1958. In the middle there's a casting of the Roman copy of the Venus of Knidos on display in the Museum of the Canopus.

Not far from the small temple, at the back of a narrow lane to the right, are the ruins of the **Gymnasium** (35). Finally, about 100 m. to the left, the small **Greek Theater** (36), with a diameter of only 36 m., still preserves parts of the stalls and the proscenium.

Ancient Roman Fountain.

The Temple of Venus.

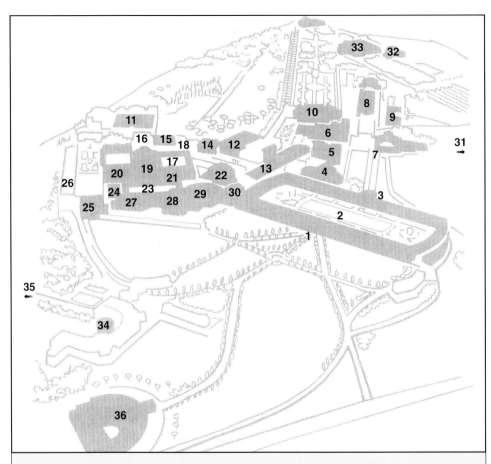

PLASTIC OF HADRIAN'S VILLA

1) Plastic.
2) The Poecile.
3) Hundred Tiny Rooms.
4) Building with three exedras.
5) Small Thermae.
6) Great Thermae.
7) The Vestibule.
8) The Canopus.
9) The Museum.
10) "Praetorium".
11) Golden Square.
12) Quadriporticus with Fish Pond.

13) Nymphaeum.
14) The Firemen's Barracks.
15) Room of the Doric Pilasters.
16) Nymphaeum.
17) Peristyle of the imperial palace.
18) Summer Triclinium.
19) Private Library.
20) The Room with three naves.
21) The Cryptoporticus.
22) Thermae with Heliocaminus.
23) The Library Courtyard.
24) Hospitalia (or Guest rooms).

25) Tricliniums.
26) The Pavillon of Tempe.
27) Greek Library.
28) Latin Library.
29) The Villa of the Island
30) The Philosophers' Room.
31) The Tower of Roccabruna.
32) The Academy.
33) The Academy of Venus.
34) Small Circular Temple.
35) The Gymnasium.
36) Greek Theater.

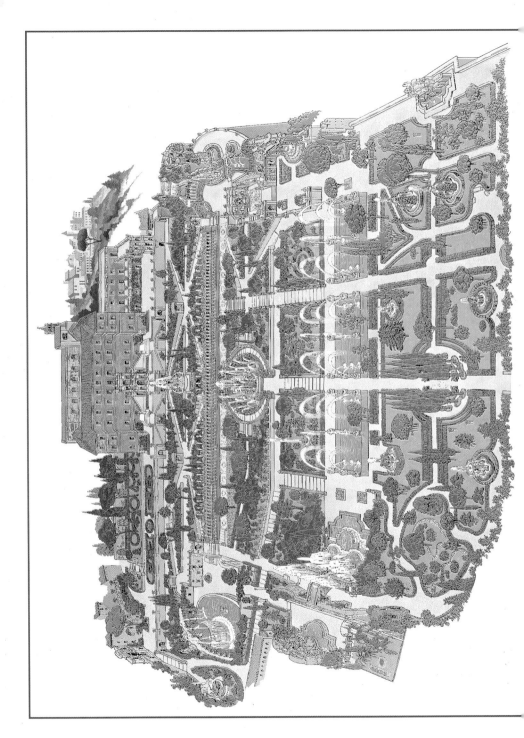

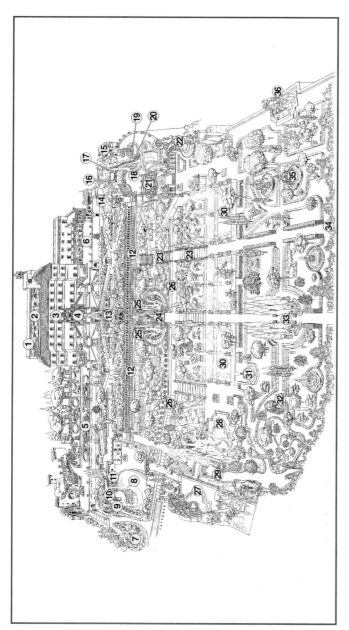

1. Church of Santa Maria Maggiore; 2. Courtyard with a fountain of Venus; 3. The Palace; 4. The staircases; 5. The terrace; 6. Courtyard of Pallacorda; 7. The Pegasus fountain; 8. The Ovato fountain; 9. The Sibyl Albunea; 10. The Aniene statue; 11. The fountain of Baccus; 12. The Hundred fountains; 13. The fountain of "Bicchierone"; 14. The Grotto of Diana; 15. The Rometta; 16. The Aniene; 17. The Tiber; 18. The Tiberina Island; 19. The statue of Rome; 20. The Capitoline She-Wolf; 21. The fountain of Proserpina; 22. The fountain of the Owl; 23. The "Bollori" stairs; 24. The fountain of Dragons; 25. The fountain of the Sphinx; 26. Via delle Ortensie; 27. The fountain of the Organ; 28. The fountain of Neptune; 29. The grottoes; 30. The Fish Ponds; 31. The fountain of the Eagles; 32. The fountain of the Prophet; 33. The rotunda of the Cypresses; 34 The fountain of the Nature; 35. The fountain of the Mete; 36. The fountain of Ariadne.

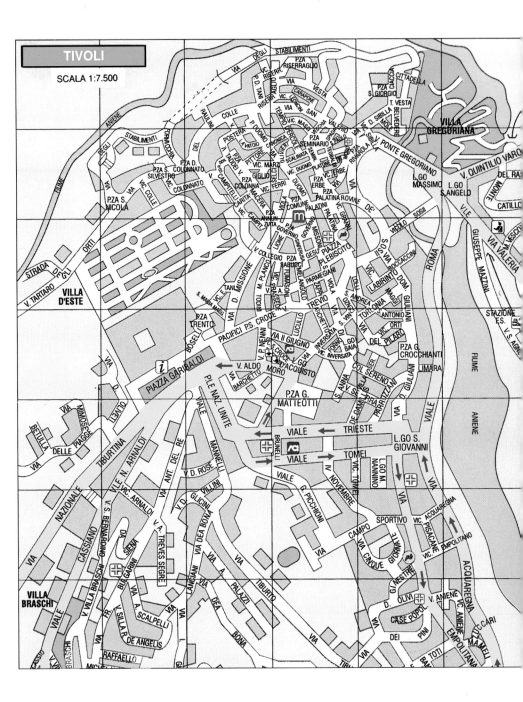